The Secrets of Easter Island

T0313583

Contents

Written by Rob Alcraft

Collins

1 The mystery of Easter Island

On a tiny, faraway island, in the middle of the Pacific Ocean, stand hundreds of giant stone statues. Made long ago, they hold secrets from the past.

Why were these massive statues made? How were they moved? What did people believe about these stone giants? Can evidence dug from the soil of the island itself, and the stories passed down by the island's people, help us solve these mysteries?

2 A land far away

Easter Island is one of the most remote **inhabited** places on Earth. The island is tiny – just 23 kilometres long and 11 kilometres wide.

Easter Island is the name given to the island by the first European explorers who arrived on Easter Day in 1722. Today, the island is part of Chile, which calls it Isla de Pascua. But there is another name too, which many people use – Rapa Nui. This is the **Polynesian** name for the island, and for the island's people.

EUROPE

AFRICA

This is a map of the world showing Easter Island. It is a long way from anywhere. The next island is over 1,700 kilometres away. The nearest land is South America, 3,700 kilometres to the east.

This is Easter Island. The giant craters are old volcanoes that erupted long ago, growing up from the seabed to form the island.

ASIA

NORTH
AMERICA

PACIFIC

OCEAN

SOUTH
AMERICA

AUSTRALIA

O C E A N I A

Easter
Island

CHILE

NEW ZEALAND

ANTARCTICA

There are almost 1,000 giant stone statues on Easter Island. A few of the statues stand only as tall as a person, but many are giants, taller than a house. Some weigh over 80 tonnes – more than two large lorries.

Each stone giant is carved from one large piece of rock – the same volcanic rock that forms the island. Each statue is different, but carved with the same strong features and large, oversized head. There is nothing quite like the Easter Island statues anywhere else on Earth.

Some of the giant statues still have blocks of red rock on their heads. These are thought to represent crowns of hair, tied up in a topknot.

This is a map of Easter Island showing the volcanoes and the stone giants – which the Rapa Nui people call "moai", meaning "statue" in English.

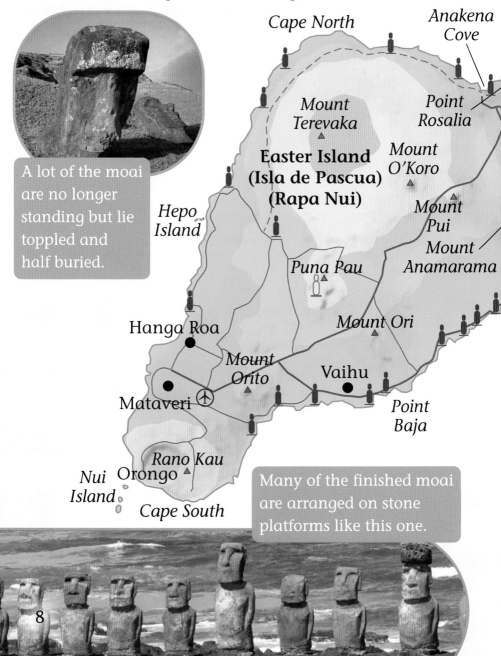

A lot of the moai are no longer standing but lie toppled and half buried.

Cape North

Anakena Cove

Mount Terevaka

Point Rosalia

Easter Island (Isla de Pascua) (Rapa Nui)

Mount O'Koro

Hepo Island

Mount Pui

Mount Anamarama

Puna Pau

Hanga Roa

Mount Ori

Mount Orito

Vaihu

Mataveri

Point Baja

Rano Kau

Nui Island

Orongo

Cape South

Many of the finished moai are arranged on stone platforms like this one.

8

Nearly all the moai are made from rock that comes from one **quarry** on the slopes of the Rano Raraku volcano.

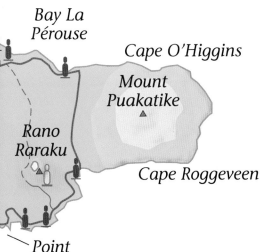

Bay La Pérouse

Cape O'Higgins

Mount Puakatike

Rano Raraku

Cape Roggeveen

Point Cuidado

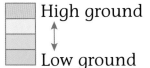
High ground

Low ground

▲ Volcano (not active)

○ Lake

● Town/village

✕ Roads and tracks

⊕ Airport

⚑ Main moai sites

⌂ Quarry

These are the slopes beneath the quarry. About 350 giant statues are still here. Over time, eroding soil from the volcano has almost buried them. But why were they left here, so near to the quarry? Were they waiting their turn to be moved?

9

Easter Island's statue-building **culture** thrived for hundreds of years, and it is thought that 3,000 or 4,000 people lived on the island. But then, in 1722, explorers and sailors began to come to the island from Europe, and life on the island began to change for the worse. The Europeans carried diseases that were completely new to Easter Island and many people died. Then traders of enslaved people came and took many islanders away. Finally, settlers came and took the Rapa Nui people's land.

By 1877, settlers had turned Easter Island into a sheep farm. Those Rapa Nui people who could, left to live on another Pacific island called Tahiti. Only about 100 Rapa Nui people remained on Easter Island.

The Rapa Nui people are Polynesians, who came originally from other islands far away across the Pacific. They travelled in large sailing canoes, like the one pictured here in a drawing of Tahiti.

Eventually, the Rapa Nui people left on the island were too young to have been a part of creating the island's statues. They had to rely on the information passed down to them from their **ancestors.**

Easter Island became a place of mysteries.
Why did people make these giant statues?
What did they mean?

Over 150 years ago, one of the Easter Island statues was put on a ship and taken away. Islanders told those taking the statue that it had a name in the Rapa Nui language, "Hoa Hakananai'a".

We know now that this name means something like "lost friend". Was this an old name for the statue, or a new one that showed what the islanders felt?

The Rapa Nui people's writing is called Rongorongo. It may tell stories of the island's history and people, but we can't be sure because no one can now read it.

3 Uncovering a lost past

Experts have spent many years trying to piece together the story of Easter Island. But how is it possible to find out about the past if everyone from the time is no longer alive?

One important kind of evidence about the giant stone statues are the stories the island's Rapa Nui people tell of. They can tell us something about the past, and what the statues meant.

But these stories don't tell us everything. One problem is that some of the stories were first written down by visitors who did not really know the island, or its language very well. It means bits of the stories are missing, and other things are mixed up.

This photograph is from 1914. It was taken by an early **expedition** to Easter Island that collected and wrote down some of the Rapa Nui people's spoken history. There were still people alive from the time before traders of enslaved people came, and before settlers took away the islanders' land. These people knew the island's history, some events, stories and names from the ancient Rapa Nui culture.

There is also evidence about Easter Island's past in the diaries and reports of the explorers and sailors who first visited the island. They made drawings and wrote about what they saw.

But this written history doesn't tell us everything either. None of the early visitors stayed more than a few days, or spoke the Rapa Nui language. How reliable would their evidence be?

This is a drawing made after a visit of just 11 hours to Easter Island by French explorers in 1768. But is this really what it was like? Another European explorer, who visited two years later, wrote of how the islanders placed great importance on the moai and were "displeased when we approach to examine them closely".

What do you think this picture shows?

Another important way of finding evidence about Easter Island's past has been to dig down into the soil itself: this is called archaeology.

On Easter Island, archaeologists have dug at important sites and uncovered bits of charcoal, bone, shell and stone. What could these discoveries tell us about the past? Could they give us clues about how people lived – and about what the stone giants meant to them?

Below is an **excavation** of one of the stone giants in the 1950s. Digging down like this through the layers of soil is a bit like going back in time. The top layers are the newest and show the island's recent history. The deepest layers hold clues about the island's most ancient past.

Like pieces of a puzzle, the different kinds of evidence from Easter Island can be compared and considered to give us answers about the past – and suggest new questions.

When, for instance, were the stone giants made? The first visitors and explorers thought the moai must be very ancient, mostly because they did not think the Rapa Nui people they met could have made or moved the moai – but were they right?

By carefully sifting through layers of soil at important sites, archaeologists have discovered that the first statues were probably carved around 750 years ago, and were in fact still being made up until around 50 years before the arrival of the first Europeans.

An experiment to show how the Rapa Nui are thought to have moved the moai.

By digging away the soil from around the stone giants, archaeologists have begun to reveal their secrets.

4 The mystery of the stone giants

Why were the stone giants made?

Each statue was a huge investment of work and time, so they must have been important. So what did the moai mean, or represent?

Early accounts from European visitors describe how many of the statues stood in groups on large stone platforms, with their backs to the sea. People, painted all over with white, tended to them. At least some of the stone giants were guarded with rings of stones – and each one had a name. Were these stone gods, or something else? Can the Rapa Nui's oral tradition help us to understand their meaning?

Archaeologists have studied platforms like this one, and have discovered they were often used, altered and rebuilt over many generations. The statues themselves were sometimes moved, or replaced, or had carvings and symbols added.

The statues' names give us clues about what the stone giants, and the platforms, meant to the Rapa Nui. The English explorer Captain Cook, who visited Easter Island in 1774, was told some of these names, and also that each had been a chief or leader. He was also told that each statue was a kind of living thing.

More recently, archaeologists have found fragments of carved bone, and bits of leftover charcoal from fires, near the stone giants and platforms. This evidence tells a story of ritual and celebration, and sometimes also of burials. Were these platforms sacred places? Could each moai have represented a leader from long ago, with their back to the sea, watching over the people and their island?

Archaeologists have found the remains of long, boat-shaped houses near the stone giants and the platforms. These sites were part of the villages people lived in, and part of everyday life.

Perhaps the most important clue about what the moai meant comes from the cultures of other Polynesian islands where the Rapa Nui people originally came from. In these other places, ancestors are honoured and remembered. Is it possible that the Easter Island people brought these beliefs with them, and thought about their ancestors in a similar way?

Wooden carvings like this female figure from Easter Island may have been thought of in a similar way to the giant moai.

The Rapa Nui people's stories tell of how the first statue was brought from far away, and that it had the power to protect. The moais were given different appearances and characteristics to match the ancestor they represented, and that each moai was seen as a living spirit, with a power to protect and guide the living.

New discoveries about the moai are still being made. Mysterious fragments of **coral** weren't thought important – until one team of archaeologists began to piece them together – and found that they were eyes. The Rapa Nui's stories tell us that placing the eyes was an important ritual that "woke" an ancestor and gave the statue its power.

How were the stone giants moved?

If the moai represented powerful ancestors, it explains why they were made and placed around Easter Island – but not *how*. These stone giants are huge and many times taller than a human. How could they have been raised and moved?

The first explorers who saw the moai imagined the stone giants must have been moved the way they moved things on ships. It would need rope and pulley wheels, and wood for strong beams and sledges, or for logs to use as rollers.

But there weren't any of these things on Easter Island. There wasn't even a single large tree. Had there once been trees and wood? Or had the Rapa Nui discovered some other way to lift and move these huge stones?

One of the first Europeans to visit Easter Island was Jacob Roggeveen. In 1722 he wrote that "these stone figures caused us to be filled with wonder, for we could not understand how [the islanders] had been able to erect them ..."

We know from the stone used that almost all the moai were carved at one quarry. Archaeologists have discovered ancient tracks that lead away from this quarry. Could the moai have been moved along these tracks?

Another discovery by archaeologists is helping to reveal the answer to these questions. In layers of soil from the past, they have found tiny grains of tree **pollen**. Did the island once have trees after all?

This is a drawing of an Easter Island canoe made in 1786. Early visitors to the island reported there was only enough wood for a few canoes, and these were made from small sticks and pieces of wood, sewn skilfully together.

Did the statues walk?

One Rapa Nui story tells of how the stone giants had the power to walk across the island. Could this story hold an important clue from the island's past?

Archaeologists have experimented, and found that by rocking a replica statue, 18 people working as a team could "walk" it forward 100 metres in less than an hour, meaning the Rapa Nui's explanation could be the answer to the mystery.

What does the discovery of tree pollen tell us about how the stone giants were moved? Does it mean that the idea of the statues "walking" is wrong?

What many experts now think is that perhaps the Rapa Nui people used a number of ways to move the moai. Before the trees disappeared, they would have had the wood they needed, and could also have made rope from the trees to help walk the statues, as the Rapa Nui people believe they were moved.

This is one of the many moai sited below the quarry. Experts are still not sure whether they were placed there permanently, or were waiting their turn to be moved – a turn which never came.

Giant palm trees like this once covered much of Easter Island. Finding pollen in the soil – or the lack of it – tells us that the trees probably died out some time in the late 1600s, leaving Easter Island as a rocky grassland.

5 Who was the bird-person?

How would life have changed after the trees on Easter Island were gone? Did it change the way people farmed and lived?

Might it also have changed the way people saw the world, and what they believed? Was this why a new figure, half human and half bird, began to appear? This bird-person was painted in caves, carved on rocks and even added to the stone giants themselves. Who was this bird-person? What did it mean?

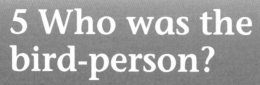

This is the bird-person, carved into a rock.

What happened to the trees?

Is it possible that the Rapa Nui people used all
the trees to make and move their stone giants? This is
one theory – but there is also evidence that it was
something else. All the seeds found from the island's
now **extinct** trees are like those shown below: they
have been gnawed by rats.

As part of the new bird-person beliefs, islanders created a sacred village called Orongo. It was built from stone, high on the rim of one of the island's volcanoes.

In the sea below the village are rocks where each spring, **migrating** birds would gather. Was it important to be close to these birds? Had they become an important source of food, now that the trees had gone?

These are the remains of stone houses at Orongo.

This is a carving of a **porpoise** from Easter Island. Bones found on the island show that fish and sea animals were a large part of the Rapa Nui people's diet – until the trees disappeared. With no big trees for wood, people could not build sea-going canoes and catch large fish in the deep sea.

Rapa Nui stories give us clues about the importance of the bird-person. They tell of how, each spring, the Rapa Nui people would gather at Orongo for a festival. They celebrated the bird-person as a creator spirit that drew birds to nest on Easter Island, bringing food and renewing life.

During the festival, the different clans or extended families would stage a contest. This was a race to bring back an egg from the offshore rocks below the volcano.

Shown on these pages is the view towards Orongo and the rocks where the race for an egg took place. The first contestant to come back won, and their family would be leaders for the next year. Some experts think that this dangerous race was a way of sharing food and power and keeping the peace between islanders.

Did the Rapa Nui people stop making moai like this one on the right because they no longer had a way of moving them? Or did they stop because losing the island's trees made them think of the world and their ancestors differently? We are still not sure.

The festival at Orongo, and new beliefs about the bird-person, do not seem to mean that the moai, or people's ancestors, stopped being important. One statue was even moved up the volcano and placed inside a house in the Orongo village. Why do you think they did this?

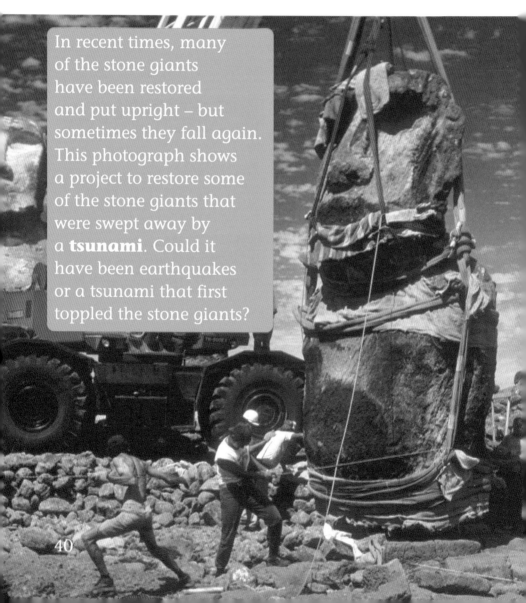

In recent times, many of the stone giants have been restored and put upright – but sometimes they fall again. This photograph shows a project to restore some of the stone giants that were swept away by a **tsunami**. Could it have been earthquakes or a tsunami that first toppled the stone giants?

But after Europeans began to arrive, things changed dramatically. By 1868, almost no stone giants were left standing. Did the disease and violence brought by the Europeans change Rapa Nui beliefs about their ancestors? We may never know – but one Rapa Nui story tells of how a woman called Nuahine Pīkea 'Uri made the statues fall, after her children left her without food. This story about anger and conflict could well describe what happened on the island.

This is the stone giant from Orongo village, though it is now in a museum. Its back is carved with bird-people and other symbols linked to the creator spirit celebrated at Orongo.

6 Island of giants

We might never solve all the mysteries of the stone giants on Easter Island, or understand completely what the Rapa Nui people believed about them, and about the bird-person. But what we do know is that on a tiny island in the middle of a vast ocean, the Rapa Nui people created some of the world's greatest pieces of stone art – not just once, but over and over again. They were organised and adapted as their island changed – and despite everything, they survived.

There are still Rapa Nui people on Easter Island today, partly descended from the few people who stayed on in 1877. The Rapa Nui culture and people live on, watched over by their giant stone ancestors.

Glossary

ancestors the people we are descended from

coral rock made by sea creatures

culture a people's ideas and way of living

excavation a dig by archaeologists

expedition a group of people that travel to study something

extinct something that no longer exists

inhabited a place that is lived in

migrating moving with the seasons, from one place to another

pollen tiny, powdery grains that swap between plants and help them make seeds

Polynesian belonging to Polynesia, a large group of islands in the Pacific Ocean

porpoise a sea animal, a bit like a dolphin

quarry a place where stone is cut and shaped

tsunami a giant wave caused by an earthquake

Index

Can you solve the Easter Island mystery?

What were some of the changes on Easter Island once the trees had gone? Here are some clues to unlock the mystery.

food

the moai

travel

buildings

beliefs

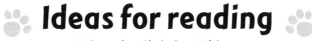 Ideas for reading

Written by Christine Whitney
Primary Literacy Consultant

Reading objectives:
- be introduced to non-fiction books that are structured in different ways
- listen to, discuss and express views about non-fiction
- retrieve and record information from non-fiction
- discuss and clarify the meanings of words

Spoken language objectives:
- participate in discussion
- speculate, hypothesise, imagine and explore ideas through talk
- ask relevant questions

Curriculum links: History: Develop an awareness of the past; Writing: Write for different purposes

Word count: 3174

Interest words: inhabited, ancestors, excavations

Resources: paper, pencils and crayons, access to the internet, recyclable materials for model building

Build a context for reading

- Ask children what they understand by the word *secrets*. Do they know any stories about *secrets*?
- Look closely at the front cover and discuss what can be seen. Read the title and ask children to suggest how these stones might be part of a *secret*.
- Read the blurb and challenge children to explain why and how these massive statues were made. You may wish to use a map to show the location of Easter Island.

Understand and apply reading strategies

- Read together up to the end of Chapter 2. Ask children to give the Polynesian name for Easter Island and to name the people who first lived there.
- On page 10 it says, *it is thought that 3,000 or 4,000 people lived on the island.* Challenge children to find three ways in which after 1722: *life on the island began to change for the worse.*